F O R

· ·

F R O M

· ·

FOCUS ON THE FAMILY®

HYMNS
— FOR A —
Kid's Heart

VOLUME TWO

Illustrations by Sergio Martinez

Bobbie Wolgemuth
Joni Eareckson Tada

CROSSWAY BOOKS · WHEATON, ILLINOIS · A DIVISION OF GOOD NEWS PUBLISHERS

Hymns for a Kid's Heart, Volume 2
Copyright © 2004 by Joni Eareckson Tada and Bobbie Wolgemuth
Published by Crossway Books
A division of Good News Publishers
1300 Crescent Street
Wheaton, Illinois 60187

Design: UDG|DesignWorks, Sisters, Oregon

Hymn quotations are generally taken from *Trinity Hymnal*, revised edition, copyright © 1990 by Great Commission Publications, Inc., Suwanee, Georgia or from *The Hymnal for Worship and Celebration*, copyright © 1986 by Word Music. All hymns are in public domain.

First printing: 2004

Printed in Italy

ISBN 1-58134-582-8 Book and CD set (sold only as a set)

All music arrangements copyright © by Larry Hall Music.

Unless otherwise indicated, all Scripture quotations are from The Holy Bible: English Standard Version, copyright © 2001 by Crossway Bibles, a division of Good News Publishers. Used by permission. All rights reserved.

LIBRARY OF CONGRESS CATALOGING-IN-PUBLICATION DATA

Tada, Joni Eareckson.
    Hymns for a kid's heart volume 2 / Joni Eareckson Tada, Bobbie Wolgemuth.
        p. cm.
    Summary: Recounts the historical and devotional stories behind the words
of many familiar Christian hymns.
    ISBN 1-58134-582-8 (hc : alk. paper)
    1. Hymns--History and criticism--Juvenile literature. [1. Hymns.] I.
Wolgemuth, Bobbie. II. Title.
BV315.T33 2003
264'.23--dc21
                                  2003002480

PBI	11	10	09	08	07	06	05	04

14   13   12   11   10   9   8   7   6   5   4   3   2   1

To my happy hymn-singers
ABBY, LUKE, ISAAC, HARPER, AND ELLA
Five bright smiles and five tender hearts for God—
you bring such joy to my world.
Bobbie Wolgemuth

For
LINCOLN REESE McCLURE
and all the hymns he'll soon learn.
Joni Eareckson Tada

S P E C I A L   T H A N K S   T O :

Mr. John Duncan
of TVP Studios, Greenville, SC,
Executive Director of the musical recording
for *Hymns for a Kid's Heart, Volume 2.*

Larry Hall, arranger

Mrs. Lynn Hodges, Children's Director

Singers:
Jane Carter, Claire and Rachael Donaldson,
Caroline Fisher, Misha Goetz, Catlin and Colton Hammond,
Mary Peyton Hodges, Abby Schrader, and Alex Taylor

We are deeply grateful for the gifts of these friends
and accomplished professionals.

The publisher's share of income from *Hymns for a Kid's Heart, Volume 2* compact disc is being
donated by Good News Publishers/Crossway Books to Joni and Friends, the worldwide
disability outreach of Joni Eareckson Tada. For more information about Joni and Friends,
please write to Joni and Friends, Post Office Box 3333, Agoura Hills, California 91301
or call 818-707-5664 or go to the website—www.joniandfriends.org

Table of Contents

Introduction

to Grown-ups Who Love Children

Portability. Because we're always on the go, it's one of the most desirable features of the things we own. From telephones to personal computers to CD players, we love being able to "take it with us wherever we go."

Because it's an instrument that goes with us everywhere, God had such a good idea when he gave us a voice to sing. It's portable pleasure, no matter how simple or talented the gift. Our spirits can be lifted at any time, in any place, and in every circumstance when we play our favorite hymns on these instruments.

In fact, recently we were wheeling and walking the hallways of a convention event, when we started harmonizing on "Onward Christian Soldiers" to liven our steps and our spirits. In no time our portable instruments had allowed us to reset our attitude and ready us for the rigors of a busy day.

When is the last time you caught yourself humming in the car or in the grocery store aisle? If you're like the two of us, you probably do this more than you realize. That voice you carry around with you is meant to be used. And there's nothing quite like humming and having words from the great hymns of the faith to pull out and play on that portable instrument.

Ever since we were little girls, someone has filled our musical memory banks with classic hymns that are ready anytime and anywhere.

My own dad, Johnny Eareckson, was the chief song leader in our family— little wonder I was proud to be his namesake, Joni Eareckson, and to harmonize happily on all my father's melodies. I remember long car trips with my parents and three sisters marking miles by making music. It really did make the time go faster.

And from my little perch on the ledge beneath the back window, (long before child-safety seats were required) I was filled with awe when I spied the majestic Rocky Mountains rising up over the horizon. That's when my daddy began to sing "Rock of Ages, cleft for me," and we girls chimed in from the backseat. I can relive those moments of pure pleasure every time I tote along one of those old family favorites. And today, there's nothing more wonderful than gathering a group of kids around me and happily harmonizing on songs about Jesus. I want to tuck the treasured hymns into their hearts so they can carry the love of Jesus with them, too.

As little Bobbie Gardner, my earliest music memory was first grade music class at Jamestown Elementary school. The words and the melody of "Glory, Glory, Hallelujah" actually made my heart beat faster. Walking home from school that afternoon, I sang the hymn over and over again, reliving that glorious moment of music that had catapulted me into another world. So strong was the longing for more moments of transport that I could hardly wait for the next music class day.

And that's just what the hearts of all children long for. They need to soar. Just as birds need air to fly and fish need water to swim, children need music to voice their spiritual longings, to voice the praise that is part of their souls. When we hand them the gift of great music, they discover the pleasure. The more truth and beauty we share with them, the more truth and beauty they have to take with them. The more they listen, the more they understand. For like time capsules, great music and lyrics continue to release over time.

And this is the reason we bring you *Hymns for a Kid's Heart, Volume Two*. For us, some of our favorite hymns of adoration and movin' along songs are these. And we have included some hymns and stories about heaven and the celebration that awaits us.

It's true. Every time we sing a hymn, we are lifting our day and everything that's a part of it to God in grateful expectation. The children you love can too. You can give them this gift that will go everywhere with them.

You can give them a picture of the goodness and the greatness of God . . .

Praise to the Lord, the Almighty, the King of creation!
O my soul, praise Him, for He is Thy health and salvation!

And teach the child you love to join you with an upward look as you move through your day . . .

We're marching to Zion, beautiful, beautiful Zion;
We're marching upward to Zion, the beautiful city of God.

And teach them the rewards for obedience and trust in His word.

While we do His good will, He abides with us still,
And with all who will trust and obey.

And, like that first-grade music teacher, you can give them a fresh prayer for America and appreciation for the God of our fathers, who paved the way for the freedom we enjoy . . .

Thy love divine hath led us in the past;
In this free land by Thee our lot is cast;
Be Thou our Ruler, Guardian, Guide, and Stay;
Thy word our law, Thy paths our chosen way.

We invite you to enter through the doorway of beautiful music, the classic hymns of the past, into the full and unlimited presence of the Creator of life . . . and music. And we invite you to plant the seeds of the hymns' messages, as well as the inspirational stories of the men and women who wrote them, in the tender soil of a child's heart. You will be giving him or her a portable treasure that he or she can carry for a lifetime.

Thee will I cherish, Thee will I honor,
Thou, my soul's glory, joy, and crown.

Joni Eareckson Tada   Bobbie Wolgemuth
Agoura Hills, California   *Orlando, Florida*

Hymns About God

Praise to the Lord, the Almighty, the King of Creation!

O my soul, praise Him, for He is thy health and salvation!

All ye who hear, now to His temple draw near

Join me in glad adoration!

The Boy Who Changed His Ways

JOACHIM NEANDER, 1650-1680

In Germany long ago there lived a stubborn and rebellious young man named Joachim Neander. Although Joachim was very bright, he fell into the wicked practices of the friends he chose. Just like today, there were schoolmates then who were coarse and sarcastic. His friends did not follow God's ways in their behavior and encouraged unkind pranks.

One day several of the boys, including Joachim, heard that a famous preacher was coming to town. The sassy boys decided to go hear the man of God. They intended to scoff at him. They planned to trick the minister by pretending to listen, then make fun of what he said.

I don't know what happened to the other boys that day, but something amazing happened to young Joachim. He had intended to ridicule God's messenger. Instead, Joachim was touched by the message. He asked God to forgive him. That very day Joachim decided to ask Jesus to be his Savior. He changed his ways and followed God's path.

To obey God, however, was not easy. Joachim needed to do one very important thing. *He needed to find new friends.* That would take courage. Finding new companions who would help him honor God and spend his time wisely was his one wish. He knew he couldn't do this on his own. He asked God to help him.

It is marvelous how God answered Joachim's prayer. There were some noble and good boys who had told their dads that they needed someone to help them understand difficult school assignments. Because Joachim was so smart and such an excellent student, he was asked to be an after-school tutor to the boys. The new, good friends were happy to study with Joachim. They told Joachim how happy they were that God had sent such a smart fellow to help them study for tests.

Good friends who made wise choices—what a great answer to *all* his prayers. God certainly loves to answer prayers of young people who try to follow His ways.

At the same time that these new friends came his way, Joachim began listening to great music. He would spend hours listening to classical music. It stirred his heart. He seemed to hear things that few others could. He would take walks next to the river and look up at the hills. Everything was more beautiful that he ever remembered seeing it before. All the world seemed full of radiant color and vibrant sounds.

It wasn't long until Joachim started to write down the words and music he felt in his heart. His friends couldn't believe it. The words were so grand that they said he was a genius. Joachim knew that the ideas came from God, and he never bragged about it

Because God's message had changed his heart when he was young, Joachim Neander grew up to give the world a glorious song. He wrote the majestic hymn, "Praise to the Lord, the Almighty," which is one of the finest songs you will ever hear.

Imagine what we would be missing if Joachim had never traded his rebellious ways and naughty friends for new, good ones. We can all be glad that the young rebel asked God to clean up his heart. God gave him a new and grateful attitude. Every verse in this hymn begins with "Praise to the Lord." That's because the best way to say, "Thank You" to God is to praise Him.

You can choose good friends and good music just like Joachim did. A hymn of praise is like a good friend who follows you around all day and helps you to be wise. And when you sing it, watch for wonderful things to happen. Praise the Lord! He is an amazing, great, and powerful friend.

BOBBIE WOLGEMUTH

Hanging on to the Goodness of God

It was a dull Saturday afternoon, and I was feeling pretty low. I was having trouble sitting in my wheelchair—my corset (something I wear around my middle to help me breathe) was digging into my ribs. It was forcing me to draw deep breaths every now and then. Whenever I breathed hard, I would say, "The Lord is good." Somewhere after the fifth "The Lord is good," my friend turned and gave me a good-natured dig, asking, "What are you doing, Joni? Trying to convince yourself the Lord is good?"

"You've got it," I replied with a smile. It's not that I doubted God's goodness that Saturday. I simply knew I had to keep reminding my dry, droopy soul of the truth. King David, the psalmist, had to grab his soul and give it a good shake every now and then. Whenever he was feeling sad, he would say to himself, "Why are you cast down, O my soul, and why are you in turmoil within me? Hope in God; for I shall again praise him, my salvation and my God" (Psalm 42:5-6).

I want to be like King David. To be honest, I force myself to be like him. When I feel sad, I know that's the best time to give my soul "a good talking to!" I need to remind my soul with the words to our hymn today, "O my soul, praise Him, for He is thy health and salvation!" It's easy to say that God is good when you're feeling great. But it's another thing—a more God-glorifying thing—to say (and sing) out loud that God is good when you're feeling low.

The next time you're feeling a little blue, remember to "talk" to your soul. In fact, use the words to "Praise to the Lord, the Almighty" to tell your soul wonderful things about God. It'll thank you for the reminder!

JONI EARECKSON TADA

Praise to the Lord, the Almighty

Praise to the Lord, the Al-might-y, the King of cre-a-tion!

O my soul praise Him, for He is thy health and sal-va-tion!

All ye who hear, now to His tem-ple draw near,

join me in glad ad-o-ra-tion.

Based on Psalm 103
Joachim Neander, 1680
Trans. by Catherine Winkworth, 1863

Straslund Gesangbuch, 1665

2. Praise to the Lord, who o'er all things so wondrously reigneth,
   Shelters thee under His wings, yea, so gently sustaineth!+
   Hast thou not seen how thy desires e'er have been
   Granted in what He ordaineth?+

3. Praise to the Lord, who doth prosper+ thy work and defend thee!
   Surely His goodness and mercy here daily attend thee;
   Ponder anew+ what the Almighty can do, if with His love He befriend thee.

4. Praise to the Lord, who with marvelous wisdom hath made thee,
   Decked+ thee with health, and with loving hand guided and stayed+ thee.
   How oft in grief hath not He brought thee relief,
   Spreading His wings to o'ershade thee!

5. Praise to the Lord! O let all that is in me adore Him!
   All that hath life and breath, come now with praises before Him!
   Let the amen sound from His people again; gladly fore'er we adore Him.

+ All words marked in this way are defined in the " Do You Know What It Means?" section at the back of this book.

A Verse for My Heart

If anyone is in Christ, he is a new creation. The old is
passed away, behold, the new has come.—2 Corinthians 5:17

Prayer from My Heart

Father in Heaven, my heart is full of praise to You. Everything I want
is found in Your plan for my life. Help me to chose good friends.
Thank You for a hymn to keep my heart close to You all day long.
I want to be wise and praise You. Amen.

Singing in Secret

ANONYMOUS, 1677

Do you know what a POW is? The letters stand for "prisoner of war." During times of national conflict, soldiers who are captured by their enemies are held in a prison until their friends find them and release them. Soldiers who were POWs in past wars have told us stories of being alone day and night for weeks, months, and even years. What do you think kept them alive in dark prison cells when they saw no friendly faces and heard no kind words? What would you do for hours and hours while you were waiting to be rescued?

Some of the prisoners who were set free have told us what helped keep them alive. It is the one thing that even the meanest enemy cannot stop their captives from doing. They could *sing* a song. That's right. Singing songs and quiet hymns have filled prison cells for thousands of years. Yes, singing in secret can keep you alive.

There is a true story of some children who learned to sing in secret. It happened in the country of Germany very long ago. Many Christians were being hunted down and put in prison. They had listened to the teachings of a man named John Hus. They believed in the simple message of Jesus from the Sermon on the Mount. (You can find the words to the Sermon on the Mount in your Bible in Matthew 5, 6, and 7.)

These believers called themselves "the Brotherhood" because they were like a big family. They loved God, and they sang all the time. They sang so much that they became known as "the singing Brethren."

Their leader, John Hus, had been put in prison and cruelly held down with heavy chains. He sang hymns in his prison cell. He was a POW who was told he would be killed. But he just kept singing. He even sang out loud when wicked people tied his feet to a log and set the wood on fire. As the flames encircled his feet, John Hus was calm. The last sound his friends heard from him was his voice singing a hymn. Then they watched as all two hundred of his Christian books were thrown into the fire with him.

With John Hus dead and all of his books burned, his enemies thought they had stopped the message of Jesus from being spread. But the good news didn't stop because John Hus was dead. "The singing Brethren" had taught their children hymns. Truthful words and beautiful tunes from the hymns gave strength to the followers of Christ, young and old. Meeting in secret places whenever they could, the people sang together and reminded each other to keep their faith in God strong. If ever they were sad or alone, they knew what to do. They sang hymns like "Fairest Lord Jesus."

Fearing that their hiding-places would be found, fathers and mothers moved out of the dangerous cities to remote villages. They sang as they walked to their new towns, where they became farmers or weavers+ or cobblers.+ As they worked, they sang the sweet hymns and told Bible stories to their children. The children memorized the stories and the hymns. This is how the good news of the Christian faith was passed on and on for generations. Over two hundred and fifty years passed, and children were still singing the cherished hymns.

After many generations a visitor came to a meeting in one of the German villages. He heard some children singing "Fairest Lord Jesus." Thinking that it was one of the most beautiful hymns he had ever heard, the man asked the children to sing it again. Quickly he wrote down the words and memorized the tune. The gentle hymn traveled with the man back to his home, and he showed it to someone who immediately printed it in a songbook. In no time the song was on the lips of children all over the world. No one ever really knew who wrote it. But that didn't seem to matter.

Just like the POWs who were kept alive by singing hymns, someone long ago sang "Fairest Lord Jesus" in secret to their children. And *they* sang it in secret to *their* children. And *their* children kept singing it until the day finally came when it did not have to be sung in secret anymore. Someday you may be able to sing this beautiful hymn to your children. When you do, remember to tell them about the children who sang it in secret many centuries ago.

BOBBIE WOLGEMUTH

From My Heart to Yours

Ruler of All

I love the outdoors. Often during summer, after dinner and dessert, my family would sit in the backyard and watch the sun go down. "There it goes," my sister Kathy would say. "There's just a little tip of light left; see it?" My sisters and I would compete as to who would be the last one to see the sun set. It was fun to watch the sun go down, the colors in the sky fade, and the stars begin to shine. After it became dark, my dad would often light a fire in the backyard pit, and he'd lead us in singing hymns.

We'd count the constellations as we'd sing. "Who can find the Big Dipper?" Daddy would ask. "Over there!" My sister Jay would jump to her feet and point. "And Orion?" "I see it, I see it!" someone would say. "Who knows a hymn about the sun and the stars?" Daddy would ask. We kids would scratch our heads, trying hard to think of a hymn that talked about nature.

"Let me give you a hint," Daddy would say. "Fairest Lord Jesus, Ruler of all . . ." He'd stretch out his sentence, waiting for us to guess the next word. "I know, I know!" we'd chime in and start singing this beautiful hymn. Jesus is greater than the woodlands, the sunshine and moonlight, and all the twinkling, starry host. Why? Because He made them to show us what He is like. He made the sun and the moon to show us He's the light of the world. He made the woodlands with big, tall trees to show us His towering strength. He created the flowers—He even made the season of Spring—to show us His beauty and splendor. This is why Jesus is the Ruler of all nature. It is why He is fairer and purer above anything—or anybody—we can imagine.

And that's something to sing about!

JONI EARECKSON TADA

Fairest Lord Jesus

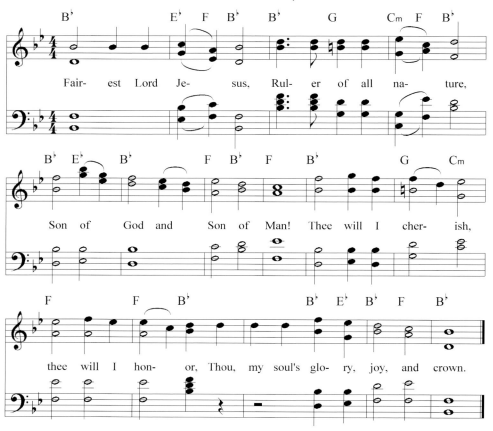

Fair- est Lord Je- sus, Rul- er of all na- ture,
Son of God and Son of Man! Thee will I cher- ish,
thee will I hon- or, Thou, my soul's glo- ry, joy, and crown.

(Children on CD sing this an octave lower.)

Anonymous German hymn
Munster Gesanbuch, 1677
Silesian folk song, Joseph A. Seiss, stanza 4

Schlesische Volkslieder, Leipzig, 1842

2. Fair are the meadows, fairer still the woodlands,
    Robed in the blooming garb⁺ of spring:
    Jesus is fairer, Jesus is purer,
    Who makes the woeful⁺ heart to sing.

3. Fair is the sunshine, fairer still the moonlight,
    And all the twinkling, starry host:⁺
    Jesus shines brighter, Jesus shines purer
    Than all the angels heav'n can boast.

4. Beautiful Savior! Lord of the nations!
    Son of God and Son of Man!
    Glory and honor, praise, adoration,
    Now and forevermore be Thine.

A Verse for My Heart

The secret things belong to the Lord our God, but the things that
are revealed belong to us and to our children forever,
that we may do all the words of this law.—Deuteronomy 29:29

A Prayer from My Heart

Fairest Lord Jesus, I cherish You and want to sing about You.
Thank You for the gift of music. No one can take away Your song
in my heart. I want to honor You and pass along Your love.
You will shine brighter than the stars forever and ever. Amen.

The Girl Who Smiled in the Dark

FANNY CROSBY, 1820-1915

Can you imagine what it would be like if you couldn't see? Being blind is like living every day in the dark. Once there was a sweet blind girl who lived her whole life in the darkness; yet she kept smiling. She had heartaches that would make almost any other girl unhappy. But not this special young lady. Her name was Frances Jane Crosby, and she became known around the world as "the sweet singer in the night."

Frances was born in 1820 to a loving couple who lived on a farm in New York. They liked to call their healthy baby girl "Fanny." But you will feel like crying when I tell you what happened. When she was only six months old, Fanny became very sick, and her parents were not able to reach the local doctor. Without knowing it, they let someone pretending to be a doctor put the wrong ointment on her newborn eyes, and Fanny became completely blind.

Something else terribly sad happened before Fanny was even old enough to talk. Her daddy died. Fanny's mother had to take a job as a maid. Fanny's grandmother, Eunice, bravely accepted the task of training and caring for baby Fanny. Both her mother and grandmother asked God for the strength they would need to guide Fanny as she grew up without eyesight and a daddy.

Grandmother Eunice took Fanny on long walks in the fields around the farmhouse, letting the little girl smell the meadow flowers and touch their soft petals. Nearby, she could dangle her feet in the cool water and hear the trickling brook. Fanny loved the friendly songs of the birds and the swoosh of the wind blowing leaves on the huge trees. When Fanny petted the little farm animals, she tried to imagine the color of their furry skin and the faces from which their playful voices came. Even without eyesight, young Fanny was filled with delight just listening and touching everything.

Listening to her grandmother's voice read hour after hour from the Bible, great classic books, and poetry was Fanny's highest joy. One day Fanny decided to try repeating the words that her grandmother had just read. Speaking phrase after phrase, young Fanny Crosby learned to memorize huge portions of the Bible. You will hardly believe it when you hear how much she knew by heart. When Fanny was only ten years old, she had memorized most of the New Testament and the first four books of the Old Testament plus Ruth and many Psalms and many verses in Proverbs!

When Fanny was eleven, she said to her grandmother, "How I wish I could go to school!" But in those days there were no schools to teach blind children, so it seemed like an impossible thing. Kneeling down beside her grandmother's rocking chair, in her bravest voice Fanny prayed, "Dear Lord, please show me how I can learn like the other children."

A well-timed surprise and the answer came the next year in the mail. Reading aloud from a letter about a new school called the New York Institute for the Blind, her mother told Fanny she could enroll there. Jumping up and down right in the middle of the kitchen, the twelve-year-old exclaimed, "This is the happiest day of my life!" You can be sure that Fanny had the widest grin on her face the next time she knelt by the rocking chair to thank God for the answer.

At the new school for the blind, Fanny's talents blossomed. She learned to play the organ, piano, guitar, and harp. Listening carefully to her teachers and book readers, Fanny also excelled as the top student in music, literature, history, and languages.

With the brightest smile, Fanny Crosby said that her greatest gift was her memory. And because she was able to remember all the Bible stories and verses she had memorized as a child, she wrote over nine thousand hymns and poems in her life. No wonder she was honored by millions of people in every land. Fanny even performed in concerts and was quick to tell everyone where her smile came from. That's why she wrote the grand hymn, "To God Be the Glory." She wanted everyone to know who had answered her prayers and her dreams.

Now it's time for you to tell someone the reason for your joy. Just like Fanny, you can tell God your impossible dreams. Then you can smile and say, "Great things He has done!"

BOBBIE WOLGEMUTH

Giving the Praise to God

Corrie ten Boom was a Christian who lived in Holland and survived the Nazi concentration camps of World War II. Nazi soldiers threw her in prison for protecting her Jewish friends and neighbors. After the war was over, she was released from the concentration camp. She was so grateful to God for the way He had protected and saved her from starvation. Corrie ten Boom started traveling all over the world to tell people about God's love and forgiveness. She became famous, and many people admired her faith in Jesus.

After she would speak at big churches, people would crowd around Corrie and say, "Oh, what a great saint of God you are," or "I'm amazed you were able to forgive the Nazi soldiers who beat you when you were in the concentration camp." These people were very kind, but Corrie felt a little embarrassed. They were trying to put her on a pedestal, and she felt uncomfortable with that. She wanted God to have all the glory.

Corrie had a plan. She decided to patiently listen to the wonderful things people would say to her, then accept each compliment as though it were a rosebud. She gathered many blessings that way, just like gathering long-stemmed roses. Every evening she remembered the nice things people said, then presented the big bouquet of praise to God. She would say, "Lord Jesus, this person was amazed I could forgive, but You are the one who forgave the most when You were on the cross." Or she would say, "Lord Jesus, a person told me today that she thought I was a great Christian, but there are no great Christians, only a great Savior." What a marvelous way to turn phrases into praises! Corrie understood that the glory, praise, and honor belonged only to the Lord. And I bet she knew our hymn, "To God Be the Glory."

JONI EARECKSON TADA

To God Be the Glory

To God be the glo- ry, great things He has done! So loved He the world that He gave us His Son, who yield- ed His life an a- tone- ment for sin, and o- pened the life- gate that all may go in. Praise the Lord, praise the Lord, let the earth hear His voice! Praise the Lord, praise the Lord, let the peo- ple re- joice! O come to the Fa- ther thro' Je- sus the Son, and give Him the glo- ry, great things He has done!

Fanny J. Crosby, 1875.

William H. Doane, 1875

2. O perfect redemption,+ the purchase of blood!+
   To ev'ry believer the promise of God; the vilest offender+ who truly believes,
   That moment from Jesus a pardon+ receives.
   Praise the Lord, praise the Lord, let the earth hear His voice!
   Praise the Lord, praise the Lord, let the people rejoice!
   O come to the Father thro' Jesus the Son,
   And give Him the glory, great things He has done!

3. Great things He has taught us, great things He has done,
   And great our rejoicing through Jesus the Son;
   But purer and higher and greater will be
   Our wonder, our transport,+ when Jesus we see.
   Praise the Lord, praise the Lord, let the earth hear His voice!
   Praise the Lord, praise the Lord, let the people rejoice!
   O come to the Father thro' Jesus the Son,
   And give Him the glory, great things He has done!

A Verse for My Heart

The LORD has done great things for us; we are glad.
—Psalm 126:3

Prayer from My Heart

Father in Heaven, You are the God of good gifts and great things.
No dream is impossible for You. Thank You for the good things You have
planned for my life. I want to smile and give You
all the glory for everything that You have done. Amen.

Hymns About Christian Living

When we walk with the Lord in the light of His Word,

What a glory He sheds on our way!

While we do His good will, He abides with us still,

And with all who will trust and obey.

Trust and obey, for there's no other way

To be happy in Jesus, but to trust and obey.

The Boy Who Spoke Up with Good Words

JOHN H. SAMMIS (1846-1919)

If you were asked to think of something delicious that you have eaten, what would it be? Perhaps you would remember a juicy watermelon or your grandmother's coconut cake. But there is something delicious that you may not think of. Words. Yes, words can taste wonderful. I'm going to tell you a story about a boy who spoke such awesome words that their sweetness is still remembered a hundred years later!

It happened in Massachusetts during a big meeting where people had gathered to hear a famous minister named Dwight L. Moody. He was coming to town to speak about God. It was to be a special evening with lots of singing. A very talented singer and teacher from the Moody Bible Institute in Chicago was going to lead the music. His name was Daniel Towner. Mr. Moody and Mr. Towner had traveled all the way from Illinois by train. The people were excited to hear the message and sing together.

During the evening event anyone from the audience who wanted to speak was invited to come forward and tell what God meant to him or her. Several people stood up and told what they had prayed for and how God had answered their prayers. Then a brave young man stepped onto the platform and spoke the words that are still remembered today. The boy wanted everyone to know about his decision to follow God.

"I am going to trust, and I'm going to obey," were his simple words. With a bright and fearless face the boy spoke about his decision to do what God wanted him to do. He would not just settle for what felt good or seemed easy. There was something tasty and very special about those words, as you will see.

Mr. Towner couldn't forget the words that the young man had spoken. Long after the evening event, the words "trust and obey" lingered in his mind. The words tasted so sweet. He scribbled the words "Trust and Obey" on a piece of paper and sent it to his friend, Pastor John Sammis. Included was a letter telling the story about the courageous boy who stood in front of the crowd and told everyone about his faith in God.

The little words touched the minister in the same way they had the singer. It wasn't long until a song was made with the marvelous words. Pastor Sammis and Mr. Towner turned the words into a very special hymn called "Trust and Obey."

The young man who had spoken the simple words was just sharing his love for Jesus. He never could have dreamed that his words would be sung by children in the next century and in countries all over the world! Words not only taste good—they can travel too. They can last longer than a lifetime and travel faster and farther than any boy or girl can ever imagine.

When you speak God's words, you can be sure they will be healthy and good for everyone who hears them. And words can take a trip into the next century. The Bible says that God's words will last *forever.*

When you sing this hymn, remember the boy who stood up and wasn't ashamed to tell all of his friends that he would always "Trust and Obey." Are you ready for a treat? Go ahead and sprinkle this wonderful hymn on your tongue!

BOBBIE WOLGEMUTH

— 36 —

Doing What God Asks

One of the special joys I remember about being on my feet was horseback riding. And what made riding special was Augie, a big, old thoroughbred horse who knew everything there was to know about jumping. You should have seen him entering a showring! He would quietly dance and prance in one place and flick his ears backward and forward waiting for my command. I never had to tug on his reins. Whenever I wanted him to head toward the first jump, I just tightened my knees against him and—flash!—off he'd go.

Augie would canter to the first jump and fly swiftly over it. He'd flick his ears back, awaiting my directions for the next move. I'd turn him into the second jump, and he'd fly over that one, then the third, fourth, and fifth, leaping through a confusing maze of fences. Almost never did he shy away from a jump at the last second. He never balked or disobeyed.

What a wonderful horse Augie was! He never "complained" about how high the fences were. He never "questioned" the complicated pattern of jumps I expected him to hurdle. He showed no concern over how hard those big, wooden fences were. He simply loved to jump. And because he trusted my judgment with the reins, he loved to do my will.

You may sometimes feel like things are confusing and difficult. Maybe you are tempted to complain about the stuff God expects you to do. And maybe— just maybe—you are tempted to doubt the wisdom of the One who is holding the reins of your life, and you feel like disobeying. Please remember that God knows *exactly* what the course ahead is all about. He knows how high the hurdles are. He is your Rider, and He is wise beyond your imagination. So trust and obey, friend, and remember that, best of all, there's a blue-ribbon trophy waiting for you!

JONI EARECKSON TADA

Trust and Obey

When we walk with the Lord in the light of His Word, what a
glo- ry He sheds on our way! While we do His good
will, He a- bides with us still, and with all who will trust and o-
bey. Trust and o- bey, for there's no oth- er way to be
hap- py in Je- sus but to trust and o- bey.

John H. Sammis, 1887

Daniel B. Towner, 1887

2. Not a shadow can rise, not a cloud in the skies,
But His smile quickly drives it away; not a doubt or a fear, not a sigh nor a tear,
Can abide while we trust and obey. Trust and obey, for there's no other way
To be happy in Jesus, but to trust and obey.

3. Not a burden we bear, not a sorrow we share, but our toil[+] He does richly repay;
Not a grief nor a loss, not a frown or a cross,
But is blessed if we trust and obey. Trust and obey, for there's no other way
To be happy in Jesus, but to trust and obey.

4. But we never can prove the delights of His love, until all on the altar we lay;
For the favor He shows, and the joy He bestows,[+]
Are for those who will trust and obey. Trust and obey, for there's no other way
To be happy in Jesus, but to trust and obey.

5. Then in fellowship sweet we will sit at His feet,
Or we'll walk by His side in the way;
What He says we will do, where He sends we will go—
Never fear, only trust and obey. Trust and obey, for there's no other way
To be happy in Jesus, but to trust and obey.

A Verse for My Heart

How sweet are your words to my taste,
sweeter than honey to my mouth!—Psalm 119:103

Prayer from My Heart

Lord, thank You for Your words that taste good and keep me
healthy and strong. They are more delicious than anything in the world.
I want to trust and obey You. Amen.

The Barefooted Boy Who Heard a Song

PHILIP P. BLISS (1838-1876)

There was nothing Philip liked better than to listen to music. But the only music young Philip could find was the sound of his own voice or the singing of the birds and the croaking of the big bullfrogs around his tiny house. That is because Philip's family was quite poor, and there was no money for any musical instrument for him to play. As a young boy, Philip worked at a nearby lumberyard just to help to buy food for his family.

Little Philip didn't have shoes to wear. He happily went everywhere barefooted. He didn't mind not having shoes, but there *was* something he wanted more than anything else. He wished he could have some kind of musical instrument on which to play a song.

With no money to buy any real music-makers, Philip wanted something that would sound like the warble of the birds or whistle like the wind or chirp like the crickets he heard around the woods near his log cabin. He rigged up some funny-sounding gadgets with pieces of wood and odd bits of metal. Philip made a joyful noise on his home-made instruments and sang contentedly day after day.

When Philip was ten years old, he happened to walk by a house along the road and heard a curious sound. Enchanting music, unlike anything he had ever heard before, was coming from inside the house. He listened for quite a while. The barefooted boy crept closer and closer until he saw a most unusual sight inside the door of the house. Sitting on a stool, a young lady moved her fingers over what looked like black and white bars connected to a large, wooden box. It was the biggest music-maker that Philip had ever seen, and it created the most beautiful noises. Sounds like a waterfall and the harmony of a hundred crickets echoed inside the house. It was a piano, but Philip had never seen or heard a piano before! He didn't know what to call it!

Though he was a stranger, Philip stepped uninvited inside the house. The startled young woman stopped playing. Forgetting that he was a ragged intruder, Philip blurted out, "O lady, play some more!"

The fearful young woman promptly asked the barefooted boy to leave the house. And he did, apologizing for frightening the girl. But Philip never forgot the beautiful sound of that piano. "Someday," he thought, "I will learn to play a glorious instrument like that."

Even though Philip was poor, he was rich with ideas. As often as he thought up new songs, he would write them down. Then one day someone from a music company offered to buy a song. Philip chose a flute as his payment. He wanted an instrument on which to play the praises of God. Then he taught himself to play it. He was thrilled with the thin and gentle melodies that came out of his new instrument.

Full of dreams and determination and with no teachers, Philip figured out how to play several instruments. The poor boy who had once worked so hard in the lumberyard dreaming of symphony sounds loved every kind of music-maker. He never complained about practicing. All the sounds were a delight to him, and he loved to sing when he wasn't practicing on one of the instruments.

Soon people were asking him to sing and play all over the country. Every time Philip made music, he felt the pleasure of God. He was happy right down to his toes, but those toes were now covered with fine, new shoes!

Philip Bliss never forgot what it was like to be a child who was hungry for music. He wrote a whole collection of songs and put them in special books for children. And it wasn't just the kids who liked to sing them. A favorite hymn for old and young people was "Wonderful Words of Life."

In the frolicking melody you can picture the barefooted boy romping through the woods, singing with the birds, and humming with the crickets. And if you take your shoes off and let this hymn echo in your ears, you will be just like young Philip—the happiest barefooted kid around!

BOBBIE WOLGEMUTH

From My Heart to Yours

Coming Alive!

I like to write. I've enjoyed writing many books (like this one I'm helping with). But please don't think that writing comes easy for me. Oh, no. When I sit in front of a white piece of paper or a blank computer screen, I'm scared. I know what I want to say, but I don't know how to put it into words. Plus, people will read my books; this means God will hold me responsible for the things I put down on paper. I certainly don't want to lead people the wrong way—I want to point them to Jesus.

This is why before I start writing, I always ask my friend (who is helping me at the computer or who is holding the pen and paper) to take my hand and pray with me. We bow our heads, and I'll ask, "Lord Jesus, I don't have any words, but You do. Would You give me Your adjectives and adverbs, please? Would You fill my head with Your ideas, Your sentences, and Your grammar? You can think of *much* better nouns and verbs than I can; after all, You are the Word of Life, and Your words are *wonderful.*" Then my friend and I smile at one another, and we plow ahead, trusting that Jesus is filling my mind with *exactly* what He wants me to say.

Sometimes after I've written a page that zips right along with crisp, clear words, I'll stop and say, "Wow, Lord, You wrote that. Thank You!" Often I'll pause to thank Him when a wonderful word comes "out of nowhere." Jesus said in John 6:63, "The words that I have spoken are spirit and life." So if you're ever stuck in class, not knowing what to say, or if you're scratching your head, wondering what to write, ask Him! Jesus has *wonderful* words of life, all just for you.

JONI EARECKSON TADA

Wonderful Words of Life

Sing them o- ver a- gain to me, won- der- ful words of life; let me
more of their beau- ty see, won- der- ful words of life. Words of
life and beau- ty, teach me faith and du- ty;+ beau- ti- ful words,
won- der- ful words, won- der- ful words of life;
beau- ti- ful words, won- der- ful words, won- der- ful words of life.

Philip P. Bliss, 1874

Philip P. Bliss, 1874

2.   Christ, the blessed One, gives to all, wonderful words of life;
Sinner, list⁺ to the loving call, wonderful words of life.
All so freely given, wooing⁺ us to heaven:
Beautiful words, wonderful words, wonderful words of life;
Beautiful words, wonderful words, wonderful words of life.

3.   Sweetly echo the gospel call, wonderful words of life;
Offer pardon⁺ and peace to all, wonderful words of life.
Jesus, only Savior, sanctify⁺ forever:
Beautiful words, wonderful words, wonderful words of life;
Beautiful words, wonderful words, wonderful words of life.

A Verse for My Heart

"If you abide in me, and my words abide in you,
ask whatever you wish, and it will be done for you."—John 15:7

A Prayer from My Heart

Father in Heaven, thank You for Your wonderful words.
They give me life and happiness. The more I know of the Bible,
the richer I am. I want to obey everything You say. I am the happiest kid
around because You have done wonderful things. Thank You. Amen.

Heroes for God

SABINE BARING-GOULD, 1834-1924

From the time he was a small boy in England, Sabine Baring-Gould loved to read about great people. He wanted to know what made them creative and brave. He wanted to know what inspired them to paint lovely paintings and write great books and change the world for good.

Reading about great heroes of the past was hardly enough to satisfy his curiosity. So Sabine visited museums of all kinds. He was constantly asking questions about the fine paintings hanging on art gallery walls. Noticing that a lot of the beautiful oil paintings were scenes from the Bible, he started to study the Old and New Testaments. Soon he met all kinds of characters. The ones who obeyed God were his heroes.

As a teenager Sabine was bright with the kind of wisdom that comes from knowing God. His friends wondered what made him so smart. Sabine was just like his heroes in the Bible who obeyed God. He grew up to be a great student, a wonderful storyteller, and the writer of over eighty-five books. But most of all, Sabine was a great lover of God.

After college, Sabine wanted to help some children who didn't have books or museums to visit. He moved to a very poor village in England called Horbury Bridge where people lived in shoddy houses and worked all day in coal mines and factories to make enough money to buy food.

The village had no church or minister to teach the Bible, and the children had no time to attend school because they worked all day and helped their parents. Finding a small apartment, Sabine moved in and started a night school for children and adults. The upstairs he turned into a chapel for Sunday services.

News spread around town about the smart young man who was giving free lessons and teaching the Bible. Soon the rooms were jammed with students of all ages.

Villagers packed into the kitchen and sat all the way up the narrow apartment staircase, trying to catch every word the young minister said. They sang hymns and listened to Sabine tell wonderful stories from the books that he had read. They especially loved his Bible stories. They were delighted to meet all of Sabine's heroes from the Bible.

Everything in the school was going quite well until some bullies decided to visit and interrupt the classes. Sabine remembered the warriors in the Bible and knew just what to do. He asked God to send help.

When the mean boys from town kept coming by to disturb the classes, a burly and bald-headed fellow who worked in a wool factory during the day became the school guard by night. When the rough boys approached the building, the brave fellow would stand in the doorway and crack a couple of big, brown walnuts in his fist. Then, bellowing as loud as a bull, he would holler, "You boys take care and be peaceable or I'll crack your heads as I do these here nuts!" What an unexpected answer to prayer that was!

With that warning, Sabine's schoolhouse for God continued to grow. A year later the young people were invited to a great festival in a neighboring village. Without cars or transportation of any kind, the children would have to walk to attend the celebration.

Sabine knew that the kids would get tired and thought, *If only they could have something lively to sing as they walk, the trip won't seem so long.* He remembered his Bible heroes who sang as they marched in the army of the Lord. With stories of their adventures in his head, Sabine stayed up late into the night and wrote "Onward, Christian Soldiers" for the children.

Singing at the top of their lungs, the students marched all the way to the next town as they carried a cross and banners they had made. Never had there been a lighter and happier pilgrimage to the neighboring village.

If you want to make a long trip more fun, just sing "Onward, Christian Soldiers." It is such a stirring song that it will make you want to march and swing your arms. When you sing it, time will fly, and you can remember the boy who loved to sing and tell his friends about *real* heroes.

BOBBIE WOLGEMUTH

Fighting for God

Every time I see a soldier in uniform, I always give him or her a big smile. I feel, well . . . protected when I see soldiers dressed in army fatigues, shouldering heavy backpacks or rifles, and wearing combat boots. During the war in Iraq, I have seen many soldiers at airports, waiting in lines at the ticket counters, and it makes me think, *They probably have a pass from their sergeant to go home and visit their family for a few days.* Once I was in line with a soldier, and I smiled and said, "Thank you so much for all that you're doing for our country!" And you know what? The soldier smiled back and said, "It's my honor, ma'am."

I like that word "honor." When I visited West Point in New York this year, I saw the words "Duty . . . Honor . . . Country" carved into the archways and on monuments and on brass plaques. West Point is our nation's top military academy, where many soldiers are trained to serve as colonels and sergeants and so on in the U.S. Army. When you walk around the beautiful campus, you see "Duty . . . Honor . . . Country" inscribed in stone everywhere. The teachers at West Point want every young soldier to understand his or her reason for going to war. A soldier's duty is to obey—it is his honor to live a noble and pure life—and it's his country that he's defending!

It's the same for you and me as Christians. We train hard to serve in the Lord's army. And God wants us to understand that we are in a war against the devil. Our duty is to obey God—to live a life that honors and pleases Him—and to keep our focus on our heavenly country, the kingdom of God! And that's worth saluting!

JONI EARECKSON TADA

Onward, Christian Soldiers

Sabine Baring-Gould, 1865

Arthur S. Sullivan, 1871

2. At the sign of triumph Satan's host⁺ will flee; on then, Christian soldiers,
   On to victory! Hell's foundations quiver⁺ at the shout of praise:
   Children, lift your voices, loud your anthems⁺ raise. Onward, Christian soldiers,
   Marching as to war, with the cross of Jesus going on before.

3. Like a mighty army moves the church of God;
   Children, we are treading⁺ where the saints have trod;⁺ We are not divided,
   All one body we, one in hope and doctrine,⁺ one in charity.⁺ Onward,
   Christian soldiers, marching as to war, with the cross of Jesus going on before.

4. Crowns and thrones may perish, kingdoms rise and wane,⁺ but the church
   Of Jesus constant will remain; gates of hell can never 'gainst that church prevail;⁺
   We have Christ's own promise, and that cannot fail. Onward, Christian
   Soldiers, marching as to war, with the cross of Jesus going on before.

5. Onward, then, ye people, join our happy throng,⁺ blend with ours your
   Voices in the triumph song; glory, laud,⁺ and honor unto Christ the King:
   This through countless ages men and angels sing. Onward, Christian
   Soldiers, marching as to war, with the cross of Jesus going on before.

A Verse for My Heart

Finally, be strong in the Lord and in the strength of his might.
Put on the whole armor of God, that you may be able to stand against
the schemes of the devil.—Ephesians 6:10, 11

A Prayer from My Heart

Father in Heaven, You are the leader, and I am at Your command.
I know that the forces of evil will try to defeat me. Your Word is my
secret weapon. Thank You for giving me the strength I need. Amen.

Hymns About
Our Home in Heaven

Sing the wondrous love of Jesus, sing His mercy and His grace;

In the mansions bright and blessed He'll prepare for us a place.

When we all get to heaven, what a day of rejoicing that will be!

When we all see Jesus, we'll sing and shout the victory.

The Girl Who Invited Everyone to the Party

ELIZA EDMUNDS HEWITT, 1851-1920

Eliza Hewitt was almost always cheerful. Even when bad things happened to her, this bright and special girl had a way of making something good of it.

Eliza loved going to school and talking to her friends. She studied hard and became the best student in her class. When she graduated, Eliza decided to become a schoolteacher in Philadelphia. *What fun,* she thought, *to be able to work at the place I love most, with the children I adore.*

In the schoolhouse where Eliza taught, the children used pieces of slate on which to write their lessons. On the heavy gray stone they could write out and erase their chalk answers and use the slate for the next lesson.

One day something terrible and unexpected happened to Eliza. There was a student who had been misbehaving and hit Eliza with a piece of heavy slateboard. Whether the naughty boy meant harm or not, Eliza's back was terribly injured. The town doctor had to put Eliza in a burdensome body cast, and she wondered if she would ever be able to walk again.

Even though she couldn't walk or run, Eliza busied herself with reading and memorizing poetry and singing. Deciding to make the best of the unfortunate situation, Eliza refused to fret and worry. If ever she started to feel sorry for herself, she would stop that thought and count her blessings. Instead of whining or grumbling, she thought about all of her good friends, her dear students, and the beautiful music and poems she was learning.

It took six months for Eliza to heal, but the warm, spring day finally arrived when the doctor was to remove the big cast from her body. Eliza surely was the happiest young lady in her town that day. She was so glad to be free that she bubbled over with the words that became a wonderful song. Guess what it was called? "There Is Sunshine in My Soul Today." She couldn't wait to celebrate with all her friends. Eliza invited her friends and students to rejoice with her. There were loud cheers and laughter for the happy occasion. It was a party they never forgot.

It was grand to be free from the cast. Eliza enjoyed walking in the park near her home and teaching at the schoolhouse again. Years later she still remembered how good it felt. One day she thought about how splendid heaven must be. She wondered, *What will it be like when broken and hurt bodies on earth are finally free from pain?* Eliza knew from reading the Bible that people who believe in the Lord Jesus will someday be given a new body and will live in the brightest, most wonderful place with Jesus and the angels.

Eliza couldn't stop thinking of people who were sick or crippled and how they would someday be running on streets of gold. *What will their faces look like when they catch a glimpse of Jesus?* she thought. Surely they would be the brightest faces! Like hers had been when the doctor removed her cast.

Eliza let her mind go over and over the idea. She pictured the big party that was being prepared in heaven. There would be singing and dancing and shouts of victory. Everyone would be arriving through huge gates that are covered with jewels and real pearls. Eliza couldn't wait to tell her friends and students about the scene in heaven. She wrote a poem about the big day that became a delightful song. It was called "When We All Get to Heaven," and everyone who heard it was overjoyed.

Just like Eliza, you and I can sing no matter what happens to us. We can count our blessings and think about the good things we have. But the most exciting reason of all to rejoice is our personal invitation to God's heavenly party. It will be the grandest party ever, and all the angels will be shouting, "Hip, hip, hooray!" when we walk through the gates.

Do you want to invite your friends to the celebration? Tell them the good news with a song. When you sing about the love of Jesus, you'll have a happier heart, no matter what happens.

BOBBIE WOLGEMUTH

Our True Home

O ne of my favorite memories as a little girl was playing late-afternoon tag in the woods beyond our backyard with my sister Kathy and our neighborhood friends. We would call to each other, and our shouts would echo through the tall oak trees. Everything echoed—the chatter of birds, the buzz of a lawn mower up the street, and the sound of garage doors opening as dads came home from work. Our play was so much fun that an hour would go by and we'd hardly know it.

Finally Kathy and I would hear Mom calling, "Girls, it's time for dinner. Time to come home!" Then she'd ring the dinner bell by the back door—*ding-ding-a-ling-ding*—and she'd call again, "Come home!" Hearing my mommy's voice would almost make me cry. Maybe it was the echo of the bell and her words… or knowing she was cooking fried chicken and mashed potatoes … or maybe it was just being part of the family and having my own place at the supper table. Mostly I enjoyed the simple idea of going home. Home meant going to a place where I was welcomed, where I was loved and knew everybody. More than that, I knew my family wasn't complete without me—and *that* made me feel needed and very much wanted. Home was a place where I *fit*.

Just like Mom and Dad made our house feel like home, Jesus is preparing heaven that way. It's a place where you'll feel welcomed, where you'll fit. Heaven simply won't be complete without you. And when we finally all get to heaven, we'll all have a place at God's table. What a day of rejoicing that will be! When we all see Jesus, we'll sing and shout, "We're home!"

JONI EARECKSON TADA

When We All Get to Heaven

Sing the won- drous love of Je- sus, sing His mer- cy and His grace;
in the man- sions bright and bless- ed He'll pre- pare for us a place. When we
all get to heav- en, what a day of re- joic- ing that will be! When we
all see Je- sus, we'll sing and shout the vic- to- ry!

Eliza E. Hewitt

Emily D. Wilson

2. While we walk the pilgrim pathway⁺ clouds will overspread the sky;
   But when trav'ling days are over, not a shadow, not a sigh.
   When we all get to heaven, what a day of rejoicing that will be!
   When we all see Jesus, we'll sing and shout the victory.

3. Let us then be true and faithful, trusting, serving every day;
   Just one glimpse of Him in glory will the toils⁺ of life repay.
   When we all get to heaven, what a day of rejoicing that will be!
   When we all see Jesus, we'll sing and shout the victory.

4. Onward to the prize before us! Soon His beauty we'll behold;
   Soon the pearly gates will open, we shall tread⁺ the streets of gold.
   When we all get to heaven, what a day of rejoicing that will be!
   When we all see Jesus, we'll sing and shout the victory.

A Verse for My Heart

No eye has seen, nor ear heard, nor the heart of man imagined, what God
has prepared for those who love him.—1 Corinthians 2:9

A Prayer from My Heart

Lord Jesus, You are my reason to celebrate. I will keep singing,
even when things go wrong. Your joy gives me strength. Thank You
for preparing a home in heaven for Your friends. Help me
to share the good news and invite my friends to the party. Amen.

We're Marching to Zion

The Boy Who Looked Up

ISAAC WATTS, 1674-1748

D o you remember hearing about the boy in England who loved poems? His name was Isaac Watts, and he has been called "the Father of Hymns" because he wrote so many brilliant songs like "Joy to the World" and "O God, Our Help in Ages Past." He was called a genius. But life was not always easy for this boy, as you will see.

When Isaac was an infant, his father was put in prison for his beliefs and for teaching truth from the Bible at his little church. Isaac's mother would wrap baby Isaac in a blanket and go to the cold jail to visit Reverend Watts. She held the baby close to keep him warm, but some people thought that all the trips to the chilly prison were the reason Isaac was so often sick as a child.

Although his body may not have been the strongest, Isaac's young mind was filled with imagination. When he was only seven years old, Isaac wrote a clever poem using the letters from his name. This is called an *acrostic*. You may want to make one up with your own name.

I am a lump of earth.

So I've been since my birth.

Although Jehovah grace does daily give me,

As sure this monster Satan will deceive me.

Come, Lord, from Satan's claws relieve me!

If you have ever had to move to a new city, you may understand why Isaac became downhearted when he was only nine years old. Isaac liked his comfortable house, friends, and town; but sadly, his family had to move away. In the new city, Isaac's father worked in a clothing shop and started a school. Isaac liked being near his dad and so many books. He quickly learned Latin, Greek, Hebrew, and French and became a brilliant student.

But another hardship came for Isaac before his tenth birthday when he came down with a terrible disease called smallpox. Instead of going outside to play ball, poor Isaac had to stay inside and rest. Isaac was glad for his books, however, and continued to write in his journal.

In the meantime, Isaac used his energy and talent to help his church friends. He had a new song ready for them to sing for their meetings every week.

Still another test threatened Isaac when he was a teenager. Some people who were not from his church said his music was too simple and used stupid word pictures. Isaac wanted to be brave like his parents. Most boys would have stopped writing songs when they heard the critics say such hurtful things. But Isaac knew that God had given him the hymns, and he just kept on writing them for his little church.

Isaac did recover from his childhood illnesses and trials and lived a long, happy life. But he never forgot the tears of his childhood and how the Lord had given him hope. As a grown-up, Isaac made the first hymnbook for kids and wrote poems for children. One day Isaac stopped some neighborhood kids from fighting with a little poem. Leaning down so they would not miss a word, he said:

Let dogs delight to bark and bite,
For God has made them so.
But, children, you should never let
Such angry passions rise;
Your little hands were never made
To make tears in each other's eyes!

The children listened and stopped their bickering. Of course, mothers and fathers were happy about Isaac's poems, for they helped little ones to behave.

Still remembering the pain of leaving his boyhood home, Isaac wrote a song about a home that God's children would never have to leave. He thought about the lush green meadows and the lovely river that flowed through his childhood town. From these wonderful memories he wrote a poem that was made into the hymn "We're Marching to Zion." When you sing it, you can march right along, singing of the glorious home God is preparing for you in heaven. Take your marching orders from Isaac Watts. Keep looking up, be brave, and let your joys be known!

BOBBIE WOLGEMUTH

From My Heart to Yours

On the Move for Jesus

My girlfriend, Careen, and I like to memorize the words to hymns when we go on trips together. Careen is my traveling companion, and we like to fill the time at the airport or in the van or in the hotel with lots of singing.

When Careen took me on a three-week trip to Cuba and then Peru, we knew there would be days we'd feel weary and tired. After all, we were going on a journey that would take us many thousands of miles! "Let's pretend we're on a march," I said, "and every time we get into the van in the morning to go anywhere, we'll begin the day singing, 'We're marching to Zion.'"

We did just that. As we bumpity-bumped along the dirt roads of Cuba and then to Peru to deliver wheelchairs and Bibles to people in small villages, we would sing, "We're marching thro' Immanuel's ground!" It was our way of praying over the people in those countries. Often late at night when we were feeling worn-out, we'd lift our spirits and sing. Three weeks later, we had all four verses memorized! When I returned home, I learned that the White House wanted me to come to Washington, DC the next day to meet with President Bush and other leaders. I was exhausted, but I knew it was important to go. *Where will I find the energy to go back to the airport for another trip!* I worried. The answer came the next morning. I flipped open my hymn devotional book, and do you know what the song was for that very day? "We're Marching to Zion." I smiled up at God. He knew it was just the hymn I needed to keep me marching!

JONI EARECKSON TADA

We're Marching to Zion

Isaac Watts; Robert Lowry, refrain

Robert Lowry

2. Let those refuse to sing who never knew our God,
   But children of the heav'nly King, but children of the heav'nly King
   May speak their joys abroad,⁺ may speak their joys abroad.
   We're marching to Zion, beautiful, beautiful Zion;
   We're marching upward to Zion, the beautiful city of God.

3. The hill of Zion yields a thousand sacred sweets⁺
   Before we reach the heav'nly fields, before we reach the heav'nly fields
   Or walk the golden streets, or walk the golden streets.
   We're marching to Zion, beautiful, beautiful Zion;
   We're marching upward to Zion, the beautiful city of God.

4. Then let our songs abound and every tear be dry;
   We're marching thro' Immanuel's ground,⁺ we're marching thro'
      Immanuel's ground
   To fairer worlds on high, to fairer worlds on high.
   We're marching to Zion, beautiful, beautiful Zion;
   We're marching upward to Zion, the beautiful city of God.

A Verse for My Heart

Let the children of Zion rejoice in their King! . . . Let the godly
exult in glory; let them sing for joy on their beds.—Psalm 149:2, 5

A Prayer from My Heart

Father in Heaven, thank You for giving me strength and a smile when I
face tough times. Thank You for preparing a beautiful city where I can live
with You forever. Help me to live unselfishly and keep looking up. Amen.

The Girl with Heaven in Her Heart

FRANCES RIDLEY HAVERGAL, 1836-1879

You could say that Frances Ridley Havergal knew how to bring a little heaven to earth—to her family, her church, and her friends. Maybe it was because Frances thought so much about heaven and tried to listen carefully to God's voice. No one could resist her sweet disposition, because Frances thought of others and not only of herself.

Such a melodious voice had never been given to a more tenderhearted and dear girl than Frances Havergal. People loved listening to her clear, musical little voice. Frances's parents knew she had been given a wonderful gift. Music filled her home, and Frances loved to sing and harmonize with her daddy.

When Frances was old enough to read, she took music lessons and happily practiced every day. Her voice and piano teachers were just as impressed with her hard work as they were with her lovely talent. Even though she was quite young, Frances could have become a rich and famous singer. Wisely, Frances made a better choice.

Frances also loved writing poems and started singing the rhymes she composed. It would have been natural for a girl as gifted and sparkling and likable as Frances to be conceited and think only of herself. But not Frances.

Instead of bragging when people told her what a beautiful voice she had, Frances had a winsome way of turning the glory over to God. "I sing only for Jesus," she would say softly.

Frances knew she must ask God how she should use her talent. Her special concern was for people who didn't know about Jesus. Before she sang, Frances would pray for the people who would be listening.

And Frances had a generous heart. That's why she was able to bring a taste of heaven to some grown-ups in her church. Once she heard that some missionaries needed money to continue their work. Frances went home and gathered some of her most valuable possessions, including her favorite pieces of jewelry, and mailed them to the church. She tucked a little note inside the box saying that she would be extremely delighted if her treasures could be sold and the money given to the missionaries.

Because Frances unselfishly prayed for her friends, they too could feel the warmth of her heavenly heart. She would send hopeful messages and rhymes that she had written to cheer them up. Once, to celebrate the New Year, Frances sent a greeting to all her friends that read:

Another year is dawning, Dear Father, let it be,

On earth, or else in heaven, another year for Thee.

A Happy New Year! Ever Such May it Be!

Love, Frances

Wouldn't you love to get a note like that? You can imagine that everyone treasured her poem-notes. They were bright greetings from the girl who had heaven in her heart.

One of the most beautiful hymns that Frances wrote will make you want to jump right into the wide river of God's peace. "Like a River Glorious" will bring a bit of heaven into your heart. It says so many wonderful things about Jehovah God that you will find yourself counting your blessings here on earth. Then you will know a secret for bringing heaven to earth.

Yes, Frances was able to stir up a lot of joy everywhere she went. She would tell you that the best decision she made was to follow God's path instead of using her talent to bring attention to herself. And she was happy her whole life because she was following Jesus. Even though Frances lived a long time ago, her hymns can make us as happy right now. When you smile and sing this hymn, you will bring a little heaven to someone on earth!

BOBBIE WOLGEMUTH

Our Great and Gentle God

When I was little, I loved going on long car trips with my family. One of the longest trips was when we traveled west to visit my uncle. We left our home in Maryland and began driving through the mountains of Virginia. As we journeyed farther, I saw many things for the first time, like caves and gorges. Our excitement began to rise when Daddy announced, "Start looking for the biggest, widest river you will ever see in your entire life!" I knew all about rivers. The Patapsco River flowed by our farm. And we would often ice-skate on the Gwynns Falls River when it froze during winter. I couldn't imagine rivers any bigger than those two.

By the next afternoon we arrived at a scenic stop on a hill. My father pulled over on the side of the road, opened his door, and said, "Okay, girls, climb out and take your first look at the mighty Mississippi River!" I ran to the edge of the wall to see what all the excitement was about. Spread before me as far as I could see was a huge, wide river—almost a whole mile wide! Daddy explained that millions of tons of water flowed down the Mississippi, and it was over a thousand miles long. We watched it for a long time, and I was fascinated that a river so large could be so *quiet*. For as massive as the river was, it seemed almost gentle and even peaceful. "No wonder they call it 'the mighty Mississippi,'" I said.

Our hymn, "Like a River Glorious," might also be named, "Like the Mississippi, Glorious." Big, wide rivers like the Mississippi seem truly glorious. Why? We don't expect a huge river, so great and powerful, to be so peaceful and gentle. But God is like that—He is great and powerful and yet full of peace and gentleness. No wonder He's called our Mighty God!

JONI EARECKSON TADA

Like a River Glorious

Frances R. Havergal, 1874

James Mountain, 1876

2. Hidden in the hollow of His blessed hand,
   Never foe⁺ can follow, never traitor⁺ stand;
   Not a surge⁺ of worry, not a shade of care,
   Not a blast of hurry, touch the spirit there.
   Stayed upon Jehovah, hearts are fully blest,
   Finding as He promised, perfect peace and rest.

3. Ev'ry joy or trial falleth from above,
   Traced upon our dial by the Son of Love.
   We may trust Him fully, all for us to do;
   They who trust Him wholly, find Him wholly true.
   Stayed upon Jehovah, hearts are fully blest,
   Finding as He promised, perfect peace and rest.

A Verse for My Heart

Seek the things that are above, where Christ is seated
at the right hand of God. Set your minds on things that are above,
not on things that are on earth.—Colossians 3:1b-2

A Prayer from My Heart

Thank You, Lord, for the peace in heaven that flows down to earth.
Today help me think about things in heaven, where You are.
Let me bring Your joy to my family and my friends.
Please give me a heart like Yours. Amen.

Hymns of Celebration and Patriotism

God of our fathers, whose almighty hand
Leads forth in beauty all the starry band
Of shining worlds in splendor through the skies,
Our grateful songs before Thy throne arise.

The Boy Who Believed in Freedom

DANIEL CRANE ROBERTS, 1841-1907

Have you ever heard about a remarkable letter called the Declaration of Independence? It was written by Thomas Jefferson, who became our country's third president. He is the patriot who wrote, "The God who gave us life, gave us liberty at the same time."

Early in our history, America was made up of colonies that were owned by the faraway country of England. In 1776 our nation sent that special letter to tell the King of England that America was going to be a free and independent nation.

The brave men who signed the Declaration of Independence said, "This country can become a great nation once it is free." There were celebrations and parades. Church bells rang, and people cheered. It was July 4th, 1776, our nation's birthday. Every summer, on July 4th, perhaps you celebrate Independence Day by gathering with your family and friends to watch fireworks light up the night sky.

Now it's time to hear about a boy who loved the noble idea of freedom. It was not quite one hundred years later that a teenage boy named Daniel Crane Roberts read that special letter—the Declaration of Independence. Even though he was an ordinary school boy from Ohio, he read and believed what it promised. Daniel believed that all people were created equal by God. He believed that God gave them the gift of "Life, Liberty and the Pursuit of Happiness." And he believed that every person should have the privilege of choosing where to live or work and should be free to enjoy a happy life.

Sadly, not everyone in America believed that. And because of this a dreadful thing happened in our country. A terrible fight broke out, called the Civil War. As unbelievable as it sounds, some people actually wanted to buy or sell men, women, and children to work for them or others. These workers were called slaves.

Slaves were African people who were traded for money to work on large farms. They were bought like property. Some people didn't think it was wrong to own slaves to work for them. But others, like Daniel Crane Roberts, knew it was not right to buy and sell people.

The slaves felt the deepest grief a human can feel as they were taken away from their husbands, wives, or children. And yet, many of the slaves were filled with hope. They made up songs and sang in the fields as they worked for their masters and waited for the day when they would be free.

Many boys and men were willing to risk their lives and fight for the slaves who could not defend themselves. Barely out of his teenage years, Daniel decided to fight for the privileges promised by the Declaration of Independence. Even though it was very dangerous and scary, Daniel pledged his "life, fortune, and sacred honor" to end the shameful treatment of the slaves as a soldier in the Union army.

Finally, when Daniel was twenty-four years old, victory came for those who fought for liberty. The Civil War ended, and the slaves were declared free by a very wise President named Abraham Lincoln. Daniel Crane Roberts knew that God had guided the soldiers through perilous days and rejoiced with the slaves over their new freedom.

What would you do if you were told that you could live with your family after being separated for a long time? Probably just what all the slave children did after the war. You would want to jump up and down and sing and dance and hug everyone around you. That's how freedom makes you feel.

On July 4th, 1876, Daniel had a song in his heart for the hundredth anniversary of the signing of the Declaration of Independence. He wrote the hymn "God of Our Fathers" to say that God's love leads all people to freedom. He wanted everyone to know that God's rules are always the best. What a happy 100th birthday party it was for America!

Celebrate the God who fills your life with love and grace and freedom. When you sing this hymn, remember the boy who loved God and became a soldier so the slaves could be set free. Now that's a history lesson we can sing about.

BOBBIE WOLGEMUTH

Standing Bravely for Liberty

I love the way this wonderful, patriotic hymn begins. Can you hear it? Doesn't it get you excited to hear all the trumpets blowing at once? The beginning of this hymn sounds so majestic and triumphant! Like drummers beating their drums at the front of a great army. Or buglers announcing the entrance of a great king. Or the opening of the Olympics. Or the arrival of the President of the United States. "God of Our Fathers" calls us to attention!

No wonder. This great American hymn honors the faith of the great men and women who helped give birth to our nation. When our founding fathers wrote the Declaration of Independence, they stated as clearly as possible that life and liberty are gifts from God. They even wrote that it's a blessing from God that Americans are free to follow their dreams. It was scary to put this in writing. They could be put in jail for signing their names to the Declaration of Independence. They could be put to death! As these great men signed this important document, they staked their lives on what they had written, putting their trust in the highest authority they knew, "the Supreme Judge of the World."

As our country grows, it's easy to forget how precious our liberty is. As good Americans, we must keep reminding each other that our nation was founded on godly principles. And maybe this is why I love the way the bugles blast at the beginning of this hymn. The sound of the trumpets is a patriotic call. In fact, when people sing this hymn, they often rise to their feet. It's one hymn that can't be sung quietly (or even timidly). It must be sung boldly and courageously. It will take bold and courageous Christians to make sure the name of God remains in our history books. It will take someone like you, who honors God like our American forefathers did.

JONI EARECKSON TADA

God of Our Fathers

Daniel Crane Roberts, 1876

George William Warren, 1892

2. Thy love divine hath led us in the past;
    In this free land by Thee our lot is cast;[+]
    Be Thou our Ruler, Guardian, Guide, and Stay;[+]
    Thy Word our law, Thy path our chosen way.

3. From war's alarms, from deadly pestilence,[+]
    Be Thy strong arm our ever-sure defense;
    Thy true religion in our hearts increase,
    Thy bounteous[+] goodness nourish us in peace.

4. Refresh Thy people on their toilsome[+] way,
    Lead us from night to never-ending day;
    Fill all our lives with love and grace divine,
    And glory, laud,[+] and praise be ever Thine.

A Verse for My Heart

For freedom Christ has set us free; stand firm therefore, and do not submit
again to a yoke of slavery.—Galatians 5:1

A Prayer from My Heart

God of our fathers, You give us life, and You give us liberty. Your good gifts
are for everyone to enjoy. Thank You for our nation. Help me to
be courageous and to be thankful for the freedom that You give. Amen.

The Boy Who Said the Blessing

HENRY ALFORD, 1810-1871

The hymn that has become a favorite to celebrate Thanksgiving in America came from the country of England. If you like to eat turkey and enjoy the festivities of Thanksgiving Day, you will like hearing about the boy who grew up to write it.

As a young boy in England, Henry Alford was *always* on the go. He never sat idle or whined for lack of something to do. That's because Henry found every bit of hard work to be an adventure. Can you guess how he did that? He would make up stories or rhymes if he had a tiresome task to do. Or if ever he started to get bored, he would try to say aloud the verses he had memorized from his favorite poems.

No matter how difficult the work, he would keep at it until it was finished. Then Henry would come into the house and say aloud a prayer of thanksgiving. With an attitude like that, Henry made everyone in his family happy.

Henry had a tender and thankful heart like his father and grandfathers and great-grandfathers. These were some of the strong men Henry looked up to. They had been ministers. As a boy, he had seen and heard of their love for God. At meals Henry would often ask to be the one to say the blessing. Thanking God for the bounty of food was his way to let everyone know grateful he was for God's provisions.

People at his father's church were wondering if Henry would become a minister too. His father said that Henry must be strong and find out for himself what God wanted him to be when he grew up. Henry prayed that God would help him make the right choice. In the meantime, he made up his mind to study hard, read his Bible, and remember to say "thank you" prayers to God.

The season of knowing came when Henry was sixteen years old. That was when he signed a contract with God. It was a statement saying what Henry had decided to do with his life. The most permanent place he could find to write the promise was on the blank page in the front of his Bible. In his best handwriting, he inscribed,

"I do this day, in the presence of God and my own soul, renew my covenant with God, and solemnly determine henceforth to become His, and to do His work as far as in me lies." Henry Alford, 1826

Henry felt his heart flutter with freedom, like butterfly wings rising into the spring air. He would be working hard for his *Heavenly* Father! What an adventure it would surely be. *After all*, he thought, *the entire world is God's field, and He will provide everything I need to do His will.* With that, Henry stood up and thanked God for all His mighty goodness.

After graduating from college, Henry became a teacher at the Canterbury Cathedral and wrote books to help others understand the Bible. Students would say to one another, "Dean Alford is the best teacher because he makes learning an adventure." They especially liked the way Dean Alford explained stories from the Bible. Like the one about God's field that the angels will someday harvest. That's when the weeds will get thrown away, and the good grain will be put into God's storehouse. Henry Alford's stories made everyone feel like being the good grain that the angels gather for God. Anyone who wasn't working hard squirmed in his seat.

Everyone left his class wanting to dig deeper into the truth of God's Word. There was much admiration for the strong and disciplined teacher. Kids smiled when they talked about their favorite teacher. "You should hear him pray," they said admiringly, "He doesn't even sit down. He just stands up and thanks God out loud in front of everybody."

Would you like a special treat for mealtime at your house? When you sing this hymn that Henry Alford wrote, you can invite everyone to sing along. You may even decide to *stand up* when you sing it. Just like Henry Alford, you can stand up and announce, "Come, ye thankful people, come."

BOBBIE WOLGEMUTH

We Are God's Harvest

I love the Amish farms that dot the countryside along the southern edge of Pennsylvania. My Amish friend Rebecca Stoltzfus lives in this beautiful part of the country. We went for a visit once, driving down Church Lane past a couple of horse-drawn buggies. When we got to a one-room schoolhouse on the edge of a big pasture, we turned into Rebecca's driveway. She was wearing a black dress, an apron, and a white hat and was waving from the back porch with a spoon in her hand. We were right on time for a country dinner—fried chicken and mashed potatoes!

When we finished shoo-fly pie, we carried our mugs of apple cider to the backyard and sat under a colorful elm tree to enjoy the crisp afternoon air. The aroma of harvesttime, cow pastures, and cherry wood fires wafted our way. "Let's sing some hymns! Do you know any German hymns?" I asked. The Stoltzfus family and their friends made a group, all with straw hats and white head coverings. My friends and I sat opposite them and made an English-singing choir. Back and forth we sang, one hymn after the next—we in English, they in German. It was the most unusual and happy time of singing I can remember!

The afternoon was not complete, however, until we had sung, "Come, Ye Thankful People, Come." After all, these Amish friends were farmers! They knew all about raising a song of harvest home. They understood "First the blade, and then the ear, then the full corn shall appear." These hard-working men had labored all week to gather in the crops before the first frost. That's why they sang with such big smiles—their work in the field was over! And soon our work in God's field will be over. God will bring His glorious harvest—that's us—home to be with Him in heaven. That's why I'm thankful—it's why I sing with a happy smile.

JONI EARECKSON TADA

Come, Ye Thankful People, Come

Come, ye thank- ful peo- ple, come, raise the song of har- vest home:

all is safe- ly gath- ered in, ere the win- ter storms be- gin;

God, our Mak- er, doth pro- vide for our wants to be sup- plied:

come to God's own tem- ple, come, raise the song of har- vest home.

Henry Alford, 1844, 1867

George J. Elvey, 1859

2. All the world is God's own field, fruit unto His praise to yield;
   Wheat and tares+ together sown, unto joy or sorrow grown:
   First the blade, and then the ear, then the full corn shall appear:
   Lord of harvest, grant that we, wholesome grain and pure may be.

3. For the Lord our God shall come, and shall take His harvest home;
   From His field shall in that day all offenses+ purge+ away;
   Give His angels charge at last in the fire the tares to cast,
   But the fruitful ears to store in His garner+ evermore.

4. Even so, Lord, quickly come to Thy final harvest home;
   Gather Thou Thy people in, free from sorrow, free from sin;
   There forever purified, in Thy presence to abide:
   Come, with all Thine angels, come! Raise the glorious harvest home.

A Verse for My Heart

Every day I will bless you and praise your name forever and ever.
Great is the Lord, and greatly to be praised,
and his greatness is unsearchable.—Psalm 145:2-3

A Prayer from My Heart

Father in Heaven, thank You for all the provisions of life. Today I promise
to do Your work. Help me to finish difficult jobs with a grateful
heart. Then I will stand up and say the blessing of thanks. Amen.

The Boy Who Could Sing Around the World

SAMUEL FRANCIS SMITH, 1808-1895

Can you say, "Hello, my friend" in another language? If you speak French, you would say, *"Bonjour, mon ami."* In Spanish, *"Hola, mi amigo."* Isn't that fun to say? Now just think how much fun it would be to read and speak and sing in *fifteen* languages! That's exactly what Samuel Francis Smith did. And he learned those languages by listening to people and reading books. There were no computers or CDs in the 1800's to help him.

"Hallo, mein freund." One of the languages that Samuel Smith learned and understood very well was German.

Some choir directors in America wanted to start a music school and teach children the most beautiful music in the world. Finding very lovely songs in Germany, the teachers wanted someone to change the German words to English. That would take a very special talent. Because he knew how to speak both German and English, Samuel Francis Smith was ready to help them bring a great gift to American children.

That is why we can be very glad that Samuel Smith had studied all those languages. He was the right person to help them. He knew hundreds of words and how to rhyme songs in different languages. Because he was so creative, Samuel was also asked to write some new hymns for the youth choirs. And he did. He wrote one of the most outstanding songs that has ever been composed to honor the United States of America. You will enjoy hearing the story of how he wrote it.

One gloomy day about half an hour before sunset, Samuel was turning over the pages of one of the music books when his eyes rested on one spirited tune he especially liked. Glancing at the German words and seeing that they were patriotic, he instantly felt the impulse to write a hymn that the talented children of America could proudly sing about their country. *Even though other countries have kings,* he thought. *America is different. We have God as our King!*

Samuel began to hear words rushing into his head that matched the spirited tune. He wanted to write down the song quickly so he wouldn't forget the words he was hearing. But there was nothing to write on. Picking up a scrap of paper from the trash can, he took his pen and wrote as quickly as he could. Within thirty minutes, Samuel had squeezed all the verses onto a piece of paper less than three inches wide and five inches long, barely the size of a photograph. The song "My Country, 'Tis of Thee," scribbled on a bit of paper, has become one of our great national hymns.

When you sing it, you will understand why, from the first moment they heard it, the children loved his song. And so did everyone else. The song was performed by the children's concert choir in Boston for a Fourth of July celebration. In no time, children were singing "My Country, 'Tis of Thee" in schoolrooms, church services, and community meetings in every town and state. Soon everyone was singing along with the children's voices all across America. They loved singing about God's gift of liberty and freedom.

Another good thing about knowing so many languages was that it gave Samuel a special love for missionaries in faraway lands. He prayed for them and even wrote a special song to send them on their way. One year he was able to travel all around the world. Can you imagine his surprise when he heard one of the songs he had written sung in six different languages? And he sang along in every language.

One thing Samuel Francis Smith knew for sure was that wherever they live and whatever language they speak, children want to sing about their country. When we sing about our country, we can pray for people all over the world who are waiting for freedom and liberty to come to their nation too.

We live in a great land. You and I can be thankful for the gift of freedom in America. And Samuel Francis Smith could sing about that in fifteen languages. Whatever language you speak, the message is the same: God is the greatest King of all!

BOBBIE WOLGEMUTH

From My Heart to Yours

Patriotic Praise

We learned a couple of pages ago that the words to "My Country, 'Tis of Thee" were inspired from Germany, but did you know the tune is from England? This beautiful melody was first popular in England as "God Save the King" (or "God Save the Queen" if there happened to be a queen sitting on the throne). Ever since 1740, whenever an English king or queen would ascend the throne, crowds would burst into singing this anthem. It's now the National Anthem of the United Kingdom.

One time I visited England with my father. We had the honor of being in St. George's Chapel when Queen Elizabeth was there. The church was crowded, and we were so excited to be sitting up front. We couldn't wait to see the Queen enter the chapel, in all her majesty and splendor. Suddenly everyone became quiet. A door opened, a guard blew a trumpet, and there before our eyes was the Queen of England. The crowd jumped to its feet and began singing, loudly and proudly, "God save our gracious Queen, long live our noble Queen, God save the Queen."

I knew the tune, but I didn't know these words. That's when I noticed all the Englishmen around me giving funny looks at my dad. Immediately I understood why. There was Daddy, standing tall and straight, singing the American version as loudly and proudly as he could: "My country 'tis of thee, sweet land of liberty, of thee I sing." In fact, Daddy didn't even realize that he was singing the "wrong" words! I was a little embarrassed—he was drowning out the Englishmen's patriotic song about their monarchy with an American patriotic song about our liberty!

Later, over dinner, I teased Daddy a bit. But he smiled, "Even if I had known their song about their queen, I *still* would have sung our words. After all, America isn't a monarchy—it's our sweet land of liberty!" And that's worth singing about.

JONI EARECKSON TADA

My Country, 'Tis of Thee

Samuel F. Smith

Thesaurus Musicus, c. 1745

2. My native country, thee, land of the noble[+] free, thy name I love:
   I love thy rocks and rills,[+] thy woods and templed hills;[+]
   My heart with rapture[+] thrills like that above.

3. Let music swell the breeze, and ring from all the trees sweet freedom's song:
   Let mortal tongues awake, let all that breathe partake;
   Let rocks their silence break, the sound prolong.

4. Our fathers' God, to thee, Author of liberty,[+] to Thee we sing:
   Long may our land be bright with freedom's holy light;
   Protect us by Thy might, Great God, our King!

A Verse for My Heart

The Lord sits enthroned as king forever. May the Lord give strength
to his people! May the Lord bless his people with peace!—Psalm 29:10b-11

A Prayer from My Heart

Father in Heaven, You are a great God. You give the gift of freedom.
Thank You for America, our land of liberty. Today help me to honor You
with my thoughts, my song, and love for my country. Amen.

Do You Know What It Means?

Abroad: Going far away or to foreign lands.

Accord: Everyone agreeing or singing in harmony.

Anthem: A song of praise to God.

Atonement: Satisfaction given for someone's wrongdoing. Jesus died on the cross to allow people to be forgiven by God.

Bestows: Gives a gift of joy.

Bounteous: Abundant, generous.

Charity: Acting with kindness and love toward others.

Cobbler: A person who makes or mends shoes.

Decked: Covered with beautiful clothes.

Doctrine: Important beliefs that are taught.

Duty: Serving and doing what is right with the best conduct.

Foe: Our enemy—Satan and evil ones who fight against God's kingdom.

Garb: Apparel or clothing.

Garner: A big barn where grain is stored.

Happy throng: A crowded gathering of lots of happy people.

Host: A big gathering or an army.

Immanuel's ground: God's pathway on earth that leads to heaven.

Jehovah: A name for the Lord God.

Laud: To praise God with a song or hymn.

Liberty: Freedom and release from captivity or slavery.

Lifegate: The doorway that Jesus opens for believers to live in truth.

List: Listen.

Lot is cast: A decision made to follow a certain way.

Noble: Excellent and great character of a person who makes godly choices.

Offenses: Things people do that break God's laws.

Ordaineth: Something planned long ago for you.

Pardon: Forgiving and releasing a person from punishment.

Pestilence: Something very dangerous like a deadly disease.

Pilgrim pathway: Traveling through life the same way as people who love God.

Pilgrim's pride: The pride of the founders of America who loved their country.

Ponder anew: Think about it again.

Prevail: To become stronger and be victorious.

Prosper: To grow and be successful.

Purchase of blood: To buy something with the price of deep suffering, as Jesus did on the cross.

Purge: To get rid of guilt, sin, and anything undesirable.

Quiver: Shake and tremble.

Rapture: Filled with joy and delight.

Redemption: Set free and released by another person who pays the price.

Rocks and rills: Stone peaks with little brooks running along nearby.

Sacred sweets: Pleasant things that belong to God.

Sanctify: To set apart and make holy and free from sin.

Stayed: Gave you the strength to endure.

Stayed upon Jehovah: Living in complete confidence in God.

Surge: A wave of something like water that is stirred up and rolls over you.

Sustaineth: Gives you courage and keeps you strong.

Tares: Ugly weeds or useless seeds of wheat.

Templed hills: Beautiful mountains that glorify God.

Toil, toils, toilsome: Hard work.

Traitor: An unfaithful person who turns against a friend or countryman.

Transport: Carry from one place to another.

Tread, treading, trod: To walk or dance or step along with your feet.

Vilest offender: Wicked person who has the most disgusting behavior.

Wane: To grow weaker or fall.

Weaver: A person who makes fabric or yarn by lacing together threads.

Woeful: When a person is sad or miserable.

Wooing: To win someone's heart with sweetest love.

Zion: Heaven where God lives and rules.

My Personal Notes

My Personal Notes

Welcome to the Family!

Whether you received this book as a gift, borrowed it, or purchased it yourself, we're glad you read it. It's just one of the many helpful, insightful and encouraging resources produced by Focus on the Family.

In fact, that's what Focus on the Family is all about—providing inspiration, information and biblically based advice to people in all stages of life.

It began in 1977 with the vision of one man, Dr. James Dobson, a licensed psychologist and author of 18 best-selling books on marriage, parenting, and family. Alarmed by the societal, political, and economic pressures that were threatening the existence of the American family, Dr. Dobson founded Focus on the Family with one employee and a once-a-week radio broadcast aired on only 36 stations.

Now an international organization, the ministry is dedicated to preserving Judeo-Christian values and strengthening and encouraging families through the life-changing message of Jesus Christ. Focus ministries reach families worldwide through 10 separate radio broadcasts, two television news inserts, 13 publications, 18 Web sites, and a steady series of books and award-winning films and videos for people of all ages and interests.

• • •

For more information about the ministry, or if we can be of help to your family, simply write to Focus on the Family, Colorado Springs, CO 80995 or call 1-800-A-FAMILY (1-800-232-6459). Friends in Canada may write Focus on the Family, P.O. Box 9800, Stn. Terminal, Vancouver, B.C. V6B 4G3 or call 1-800-661-9800. Visit our Web site—www.family.org—to learn more about Focus on the Family or to find out if there is an associate office in your country.

We'd love to hear from you!